SIMPLY *Classics*

INTERMEDIATE

Polonaise

Frédéric Chopin

Arranged for Piano Solo by Allan Small

Alfred

The polonaise is a national dance of Chopin's native Poland. It probably originated in the Polish court in the 1500s as a stately ceremonial march and should be played quite majestically, at a moderate tempo. Many composers wrote polonaises; however, Chopin's piano compositions of this type are among the finest. Op. 53 is perhaps the best known of Chopin's polonaises.

Theme from

Polonaise

Frédéric Chopin (1810–1849)
Op. 53
Arr. Allan Small

14
19
23
27

ISBN-10: 0-7390-1260-6
ISBN-13: 978-0-7390-1260-4

9 780739 012604

alfred.

9780739012604

TP
APEX